making fresh bread

making fresh bread

CREATE FRESH BREAD IN YOUR HOME

WITH PERFECT RESULTS

Love Food ® is an imprint of Parragon Books Ltd

Parragon
Queen Street House
4 Queen Street
Bath BA1 1HE, UK

ISBN: 978-1-4075-2898-4
Printed in China

Designed by Emily Lewis
Photography by Günter Beer
Home economy by Stevan Paul
New recipes by Linda Doeser

NOTES FOR THE READER

This book uses imperial, metric, and US cup measurements. Follow the same units of measurement
throughout; do not mix imperial and metric. All spoon measurements are level: teaspoons are assumed to be
5 ml, and tablespoons are assumed to be 15 ml. Unless otherwise stated, milk is assumed to be whole, eggs
and individual vegetables, such as potatoes, are medium, and pepper is freshly ground black pepper.
The times given are an approximate guide only. Preparation times differ according to the techniques used by
different people and the cooking times may also vary from those given as a result of the type of oven used.
Optional ingredients, variations, or serving suggestions have not been included in the calculations.
Recipes using raw or very lightly cooked eggs should be avoided by infants, the elderly, pregnant women,
convalescents, and anyone with a chronic condition. Pregnant and breastfeeding women are advised to
avoid eating peanuts and peanut products. Those with nut allergies should be aware that some of the
prepared ingredients used in the recipes in this book may contain nuts. Always check the packaging
before use.

contents

introduction

Most people would agree that there are few more appetizing smells than that of freshly baked bread. A better-kept secret, however, is that rhythmically kneading bread dough is a fabulous stress buster. In other words, making and baking your own bread is a genuinely pleasurable and satisfying activity with the bonus of fabulous edible results.

Of course, these days there are bread machines available that will do all the work for you and bake the loaf as well. In light of this, it might seem that making bread by hand and baking it in a conventional oven is like reinventing the wheel. Quite apart from the feel-good factor of home baking, the answer to this criticism is that bread machines do a job but have their limitations. Only a proportion of the different kinds of bread—never mind the hundreds of different shapes—can be made satisfactorily in a bread machine. They certainly have their uses (see SHORTCUTS, page 10) but will never completely replace the keen and enthusiastic baker, whether a knowledgeable professional or an eager amateur.

It is a mistake to think that making bread dough is time-consuming, although it is true that the process cannot be rushed. What might be described as hands-on time, when you are actively mixing, kneading, or shaping the dough, is probably only about 30 minutes, but these activities are separated by much longer periods while the dough is resting or rising. So although several hours may elapse between starting and finishing the process, for quite a lot of that time you are not required in the kitchen and can get on with some other task or watch your favorite television program.

A WORD ABOUT INGREDIENTS

Given that bread is such a basic staple, it should be no surprise that the ingredients used to make it are found in most kitchens most of the time. Because they are so familiar, there is little purpose in repeating information that everyone already knows. However, there are a couple of particular points, and some guidance about cooking with yeast is also given below. Flour is probably the most important ingredient. Bread flour, whether white, brown, or whole wheat, is most commonly used in yeast doughs. It is milled from hard wheat containing a high level of the protein gluten, which is what gives the bread its texture. There is no substitute. All-purpose and

self-rising flour are mainly used for sweet breads. Of course, not all breads are made from wheat flour. Other grains, including rye, cornmeal, buckwheat, barley, and oats, feature in bread recipes all over the world.

Much has been written recently about dangerously high levels of salt in the diet and commercially produced bread has been named as one of the main culprits. Salt is not just added to the dough for additional flavor, although without any salt bread would taste extremely bland. Salt has a retardant effect on yeast—it slows down fermentation. Given that you are always told to leave the dough in a warm place to speed up rising, this might seem an odd thing to recommend. However, because salt regulates the rate of fermentation, the gluten is strengthened, preventing the dough from over-rising and collapsing. It is important, therefore, that you do not omit or reduce the quantity of salt specified in the recipes. Salt substitutes are not effective.

ALL ABOUT YEAST

Yeast is a microscopic fungus used as a raising agent in the doughs of some breads and cakes. When mixed with flour and liquid, it ferments and gives off the gas carbon dioxide, which causes the dough to rise. It is a living organism and so can be killed if handled wrongly. It functions most efficiently at a temperature of 70–97°F/21–36°C and this is why recipes emphasize that liquids added to the mixture should be lukewarm and the dough should be left to rise in a warm place. However, temperatures higher than this range will kill the yeast and the dough will never rise.

Many people are slightly nervous about using yeast and are confused because it is available in different forms. In fact, it is very easy to distinguish between the three common types of culinary yeast available and to use any of them.

Fresh yeast, sometimes called compressed yeast, is firm, moist, and creamy beige in color. Nowadays, it is quite difficult to obtain but may be available from health food stores and baker's suppliers. It can be stored for up to 2 weeks in the refrigerator. First, put it into a plastic container with a lid and punch a few holes in the lid. To activate fresh yeast, use a fork to mash it with the lukewarm liquid specified in the recipe in a bowl. A pinch of sugar may be added. Once it has formed a smooth paste, add it to the well in the center of the dry ingredients.

Dried yeast in the form of light brown, medium granules is widely available in supermarkets. Although it will keep for a very long time, it is sensible to note the expiration date on the package. If you do use it after this date, make sure that it is frothy before adding it to the other ingredients. To activate dried yeast, mix a teaspoon of sugar with the lukewarm liquid specified in the recipe in a bowl. Sprinkle the yeast over the surface and let stand for 10–15 minutes, until frothy. Stir to a paste and add to the well in the center of the dry ingredients.

Active dry yeast in the form of fine granules is available from supermarkets and grocers. It is sold in packages containing a number of envelopes, each weighing about $^1/_4$ oz/7 g, the equivalent of $2^1/_2$ teaspoons. It is the most popular type of yeast and features in many of the recipes in this book. Store it in a cool dry place and take note of the expiration date. Active dry yeast is simply added to the mixture with the flour and the other dry ingredients and does not require activating in advance.

To all intents and purposes, there is little qualitative difference between these yeasts apart from their convenience and availability. However, professionals will often insist that fresh yeast always produces the best bread, and it does have a more distinctive yeasty flavor that some people like. There is a quantitative difference and these are the equivalents (quantities required for $4^1/_2$ cups flour): $^1/_2$–1 oz/15–25 g fresh yeast = 2 tsp dried yeast = 1 envelope active dry yeast.

HOW TO KNEAD

Kneading is the process that releases the gluten in the flour to produce a smooth and elastic dough. Once a stiff, sticky dough has been mixed in the bowl, turn it out onto a lightly floured counter and gather it into a ball. Flatten and fold one half over the other, bringing the top toward you. If you are right-handed, push the dough away from you with the heel of your right hand and rotate the dough slightly toward with you with your left hand. Continue to fold the dough, push it with the heel of your hand, and rotate it slightly for 10 minutes, until it is smooth and elastic. If you are left-handed, use the heel of your left hand to push the dough and your right hand to rotate it. Stop kneading once the dough is smooth—you'll probably be glad to because it's quite hard work. Over-kneading results in bread with an uneven or very open texture.

Once the dough has doubled in volume, it is time to punch down. To do this, punch it with your fist to disperse the gas bubbles produced by the yeast.

TOP TIPS FOR THE BEST BREAD

Generally speaking, making bread is astonishingly easy, although there are some specialty breads that are best left to professionals. It's mostly a matter of common sense and following a few important guidelines.

• Before you start, make sure that you have all the ingredients listed and don't try using substitutes until you've gained a little experience.

• Always check the expiration date, particularly on flour, because it can go off, and on yeast, because it loses its potency over time.

• Have all ingredients at room temperature before you start. Liquids for yeast doughs should be lukewarm, that is, just hot to the touch. If any hotter, they will kill the yeast and the dough will not rise.

• Do not rush any of the stages, whether kneading or rising (also known as proving) because the results will be disappointing. However, there are some tried-and-tested shortcuts (see page 10).

• A yeast dough will rise more rapidly in a warm place, such as a warmed oven, but do not put the dough somewhere hot, such as directly over a radiator or next to a hot water tank, because you will kill the yeast. A yeast dough will still rise in a cooler place, even in the refrigerator—it just takes longer. If the dough has been left to rise in the refrigerator, which takes about 24 hours, let it stand at room temperature for 30 minutes before shaping.

• It is important to cover the dough when it is left to rise to make sure that it rises at a steady rate.

• Once the dough has doubled in volume, punch it down and shape it into a loaf. If it is left to rise for too long, the bread may develop a grayish crumb, smell strongly of yeast, and have a heavy feel to it.

• When shaping the dough, flour the counter only lightly. The dough should not be sticky at this stage and too much flour will spoil the color of the crust.

• Because raising agents, such as baking soda and baking powder, are activated as soon as liquid is added to the mixture, non-yeast breads should be

baked as soon as the loaves are ready and not left standing for prolonged periods.

• Most bread, especially loaves made with yeast dough, should be left to cool on a wire rack for at least 30 minutes before slicing to let the steam escape.

• Cut bread with a long, sharp serrated knife, using a sawing action to avoid damaging the delicate crumb. Stand the bread on a wooden board to avoid damaging the knife.

• Freshly baked bread should be stored in a cool dry place, but not in the refrigerator because it will go stale more quickly. Ideally, eat it within 2 days. Some breads and rolls can be frozen, sealed in a freezer bag, for up to 3 months. However, very crusty breads tend to fall apart when thawed.

THE SECRET OF AN EXTRA CRISP CRUST

Brushing the loaf with a salt-water glaze before baking and again halfway through helps produce a crisper crust. To make it, mix a pinch of salt with 2 tablespoons of water in a bowl.

Introducing steam into the oven during baking first softens the dough and then enhances caramelization of the sugars in it, producing a crisper crust. The best way to do this is to use a spray bottle to mist the walls, floor, and door of the oven with water several times during the first 10 minutes of baking. Make sure that you do not spray the heating elements, fan, or oven light. Alternatively, you can simply wipe a damp cloth over the walls, floor, and door of the oven, taking care to avoid burning your hand. A third option is to half-fill a roasting pan with water and put it into the bottom of the oven. Try one of these techniques with rustic breads, such as ciabatta.

Using a baking stone is another way to help create an extra crisp crust, because it has some of the same effect as cooking in a clay or brick oven. It is a thick, unglazed ceramic slab that will draw out moisture from the bottom of bread placed directly on it. It is mainly used for rustic breads and pizzas. Unglazed terra-cotta tiles make a good substitute. The stone or tiles should be preheated in the oven for about 30 minutes before the bread is placed directly on top. A peel—a sort of long-handled shovel used by bakers and pizza cooks—is the safest way to do this.

SHORTCUTS

• *Using a bread machine* Available in a number of sizes, these machines take all the work out of making bread. They may be used for mixing the dough, controlling its temperature while rising, and for baking the loaf. The size and shape of the pan in the bread machine limits the choice of loaf you can make. However it can be useful to use the machine for mixing, kneading, and rising before turning out the dough and shaping it by hand to bake in the oven. Bread machines are quite large and take up storage space in the kitchen. Some are very expensive. The texture of the bread is softer than that of handmade loaves. If you are going to use a bread machine, read the manufacturer's instructions carefully first.

• *Kneading with a mixer or food processor* An electric mixer with one or more dough hooks attached or a good-quality food processor speeds up the kneading process and reduces the effort involved.

• *Rising in the microwave* When the dough has been kneaded and become smooth and elastic, shape it into a ball and put it into a microwave-proof bowl without oiling it first. Cover with lightly oiled plastic wrap and heat on High for 10 seconds, then let stand for 20 minutes. If the dough has not doubled in volume, heat on High for 10 seconds more and let stand for another 10 minutes.

THE FINAL KEY TO SUCCESSFUL BREAD-MAKING

All cooking, including bread-making, is a combination of science and art. Measuring the ingredients, preheating the oven, even following the method in a recipe is the science part. The art aspect comes from getting to know instinctively just how the dough should feel when you knead it or recognizing when the color and crispness of the crust exactly match the softness of the interior crumb.

Making bread may be affected by plenty of variables, such as the temperature and humidity in the kitchen. Samples from two bags of the same brand of flour—never mind a variety of brands—may absorb different amounts of liquid. Learn to trust your senses and your instincts and, in no time, you will "just know" when the dough needs another spoonful of water or an extra sprinkling of flour to make the truly perfect loaf. And that's something a bread machine will never be able to do.

basic bread recipe

You can make two small loaves or one large loaf with this classic recipe or even shape the dough into about 12 rolls. For other variations, see right.

MAKES 1 LARGE LOAF

Ingredients
4½ cups white bread flour, plus extra for dusting
2 tsp salt
1 envelope active dry yeast
1 tbsp butter
1¼ cups lukewarm water
vegetable oil, for brushing
pinch of salt dissolved in 2 tbsp water, to glaze

1 Sift the flour and salt together into a bowl and stir in the yeast. Add the butter and rub in with your fingertips. Make a well in the center and pour in the lukewarm water. Stir well with a wooden spoon until the dough begins to come together, then knead with your hands until it leaves the side of the bowl. Turn out onto a lightly floured counter and knead well for about 10 minutes, until smooth and elastic.

2 Brush a bowl with oil. Shape the dough into a ball, put it into the bowl, and put the bowl into a plastic bag or cover with a damp dish towel. Let rise in a warm place for 1–2 hours, until the dough has doubled in volume.

3 Brush a 7½ x 4½ x 3½-in/19 x 12 x 9-cm loaf pan with oil. Turn out the dough onto a lightly floured counter and punch down with your fist. Let rest for 10 minutes, then, with a lightly floured hand, flatten the dough into a rectangle the same width as the pan. Fold it into 3 and place in the prepared pan, seam side down. Put the pan into a plastic bag or cover with a damp dish towel and let rise in a warm place for 40–80 minutes, until the dough has reached the top of the pan.

4 Meanwhile, preheat the oven to 450°F/230°C. Brush the top of the loaf with the salt-water glaze and bake for about 40 minutes, until it has shrunk from the sides of the pan, the crust is golden brown, and the loaf sounds hollow when tapped on the base with your knuckles. Turn out onto a wire rack to cool.

COOK'S TIP
If making 2 small loaves, bake for about 30 minutes. Bake rolls on a lightly oiled cookie sheet spaced 1 in/2.5 cm apart for 12–15 minutes.

VARIATIONS
- *Whole Wheat* Substitute whole wheat bread flour for half the white flour. You may need a little extra lukewarm water. This makes a nutty-flavored loaf that is not too chewy. If you want to use all whole wheat flour and not a mixture of whole wheat and white flour, add enough water to make a sticky dough and beat well with a wooden spoon. Bake the loaf for 10–20 minutes longer.
- *Crown Loaf* Make half the quantity of dough as described in step 1 and let rise as described in step 2. Brush a 6-in/15-cm diameter cake pan with oil. Punch down the dough and divide it into 6 pieces. Shape each into a roll and place 5 of them in a ring around the prepared pan. Put the remaining roll in the center. Put the pan into a plastic bag or cover with a damp dish towel and let rise in a warm place for 30 minutes. Meanwhile, preheat the oven to 450°F/230°C. Beat together 1 egg, 1 tablespoon water, and a pinch of sugar in a bowl and brush the glaze over the loaf. Bake for 25–30 minutes.
- *Milk Bread* Substitute lukewarm lowfat or whole milk for the water, depending on how rich you want the loaf to taste.
- *Enriched Bread* Lightly beat together 1 egg and 1 egg yolk in a measuring cup, then add lukewarm water to make the liquid up to 1¼ cups. Add to the dry ingredients and continue as described in the basic recipe.
- *Seed-Topped Loaf* Just before baking the bread, brush the top with 1 tablespoon milk instead of the salt-water glaze and sprinkle with 2 tablespoon seeds, such as poppy, sunflower, nigella, sesame, pumpkin, linseed, or a mixture.

traditional bread

english muffins

Ingredients

4 cups white bread flour, plus extra for dusting

½ tsp salt

1 tsp superfine sugar

1½ tsp active dry yeast

generous 1 cup lukewarm water

½ cup plain yogurt

vegetable oil, for brushing

¼ cup semolina

butter and jelly, to serve

MAKES 10–12 MUFFINS

1 Sift the flour and salt together into a bowl and stir in the sugar and yeast. Make a well in the center and add the lukewarm water and yogurt. Stir with a wooden spoon until the dough begins to come together, then knead with your hands until it comes away from the side of the bowl. Turn out onto a lightly floured counter and knead for 5–10 minutes, until smooth and elastic.

2 Brush a bowl with oil. Shape the dough into a ball, put it into the bowl, and put the bowl into a plastic bag or cover with a damp dish towel. Let rise in a warm place for 30–40 minutes, until the dough has doubled in volume.

3 Dust a cookie sheet with flour. Turn out the dough onto a lightly floured counter and knead lightly. Roll out to a thickness of ¾ inch/2 cm. Stamp out 10–12 rounds with a 3-inch/7.5-cm cookie cutter and sprinkle each round with semolina. Transfer the muffins to the prepared cookie sheet, put it into a plastic bag or cover with a damp dish towel, and let rise in a warm place for 30–40 minutes.

4 Heat a grill pan or large skillet over medium–high heat and brush lightly with oil. Add half the muffins and cook for 7–8 minutes on each side, until golden brown. Cook the remaining muffins in the same way.

5 Let cool and store in an airtight container for up to 2 days. To serve, split the muffins in half and toast lightly before serving with butter and jelly.

brioche

Ingredients

2 cups white bread flour, plus extra for dusting

½ tsp salt

1 tbsp superfine sugar

1½ tsp active dry yeast

2 eggs

2 tbsp lukewarm milk

¼ cup unsalted butter, softened, plus extra for greasing

Glaze

1 egg yolk

1 tbsp milk

MAKES 1 LOAF

1 Sift the flour and salt into a food processor and add the sugar and yeast. Lightly beat the eggs with the milk in a bowl. With the machine running, gradually add the egg-and-milk mixture and process, scraping down the sides as necessary, for 2–3 minutes, until a dough forms. Cut the butter into small pieces and add to the dough. Pulse the machine until the butter is fully incorporated.

2 Grease a bowl with butter. Shape the dough into a ball, put it into the bowl, and put the bowl into a plastic bag or cover with a damp dish towel. Let rise in a warm place for 1 hour, until the dough has doubled in volume.

3 Grease a brioche mold with butter. Turn out the dough onto a lightly floured counter and punch down gently with your fist. Cut off about a quarter of the dough and wrap in plastic wrap. Knead the larger piece of dough, shape into a ball, place in the prepared mold, and indent the top. Unwrap the smaller piece of dough, knead lightly into a pear shape, and place on top of the indent to make the tête. Put the mold into a plastic bag or cover with a damp dish towel and let rise in a warm place for 1 hour.

4 Preheat the oven to 425°F/220°C. To make the glaze, beat the egg yolk with the milk, then brush over the top of the brioche. Bake for 40–45 minutes, until golden brown. Turn out onto a wire rack to cool.

bagels

Ingredients

3 cups white bread flour, plus extra for dusting

2 tsp salt

1 envelope active dry yeast

1 tbsp lightly beaten egg

scant 1 cup lukewarm water

vegetable oil, for brushing

1 egg white

2 tbsp water

2 tbsp caraway seeds

MAKES 10 BAGELS

1 Sift the flour and salt together into a bowl and stir in the yeast. Make a well in the center, pour in the egg and lukewarm water, and mix to a dough. Turn out onto a lightly floured counter and knead well for about 10 minutes, until smooth.

2 Brush a bowl with oil. Shape the dough into a ball, place it in the bowl, and put the bowl into a plastic bag or cover with a damp dish towel. Let rise in a warm place for 1 hour, until the dough has doubled in volume.

3 Brush 2 cookie sheets with oil and dust a baking sheet with flour. Turn out the dough onto a lightly floured counter and punch down with your fist. Knead for 2 minutes, then divide into 10 pieces. Shape each piece into a ball and let rest for 5 minutes. Gently flatten each ball with a lightly floured hand and make a hole in the center with the handle of a wooden spoon. Put the bagels on the floured sheet, put it into a plastic bag or cover with a damp dish towel, and let rise in a warm place for 20 minutes.

4 Meanwhile, preheat the oven to 425°F/220°C and bring a large pan of water to a boil. Reduce the heat until the water is barely simmering, then add 2 bagels. Poach for 1 minute, then turn over, and poach for 30 seconds more. Remove with a slotted spoon and drain on a dish towel. Poach the remaining bagels in the same way.

5 Transfer the bagels to the oiled cookie sheets. Beat the egg white with 2 teaspoons of the water in a bowl and brush it over the bagels. Sprinkle with the caraway seeds and bake for 25–30 minutes, until golden brown. Transfer to a wire rack to cool.

cottage loaf

Ingredients

6 cups white bread flour, plus extra for dusting

2 tsp salt

1 envelope active dry yeast

1¾ cups lukewarm water

vegetable oil, for brushing

MAKES 1 LARGE LOAF

1 Sift the flour and salt together into a bowl. Add the yeast and stir in. Make a well in the center, pour in the lukewarm water, and stir with a wooden spoon until the dough begins to come together, then knead with your hands until it leaves the side of the bowl. Turn out onto a lightly floured counter and knead for about 10 minutes, until smooth and elastic.

2 Brush a bowl with oil. Shape the dough into a ball, put it into the bowl, and put the bowl into a plastic bag or cover with a damp dish towel. Let rise in a warm place for 1–2 hours, until the dough has doubled in volume.

3 Brush 2 cookie sheets with oil. Turn out the dough onto a lightly floured counter and punch down with your fist. Knead for 2 minutes, then divide the dough into 2 pieces, one about twice the size of the other. Shape each piece into a ball, put them onto the prepared cookie sheets, and put the cookie sheets into plastic bags or cover with damp dish towels. Let rise in a warm place for 30 minutes.

4 With a floured hand, gently flatten the larger ball of dough. Cut a 2-in/5-cm cross in the center of the top and brush with water. Put the smaller ball of dough on top. Make small vertical slashes all around both pieces of dough. Brush the handle of a wooden spoon with oil and push it into the center of the loaf so that it makes a hole through both pieces of dough. Put the loaf on the cookie sheet into a plastic bag or cover with a damp dish towel. Let stand in a warm place for 15 minutes.

5 Meanwhile, preheat the oven to 425°F/220°C. Bake the loaf for 40 minutes, until the crust is golden brown and it sounds hollow when tapped on the bottom with your knuckles. Transfer to a wire rack to cool.

mixed seed bread

Ingredients

3¼ cups white bread flour, plus extra for dusting

scant 1¼ cups rye flour

1½ tsp salt

1½ tbsp nonfat dry milk

1 tbsp light brown sugar

1 tsp active dry yeast

1½ tbsp sunflower oil, plus extra for brushing

2 tsp lemon juice

1¼ cups lukewarm water

1 tsp caraway seeds

½ tsp poppy seeds

½ tsp sesame seeds

Topping

1 egg white

1 tbsp water

1 tbsp sunflower or pumpkin seeds

MAKES 1 LOAF

1 Sift both types of flour and the salt together into a bowl and stir in the milk, sugar, and yeast. Make a well in the center and pour in the oil, lemon juice, and lukewarm water. Add the seeds. Stir well with a wooden spoon until the dough begins to come together, then knead with your hands until it leaves the side of the bowl. Turn out onto a lightly floured counter and knead well for about 10 minutes, until smooth and elastic.

2 Brush a bowl with oil. Shape the dough into a ball, put it into the bowl, and put the bowl into a plastic bag or cover with a damp dish towel. Let rise in a warm place for 1 hour, until the dough has doubled in volume.

3 Brush a 9 x 5 x 3-inch/23 x 13 x 8-cm loaf pan with oil. Turn out the dough onto a lightly floured counter, punch down with your fist, and knead for 1 minute. With lightly floured hands, shape the dough into a rectangle the same length as the pan and flatten slightly. Fold it lengthwise into 3 and place in the pan, seam side down. Put the pan into a plastic bag or cover with a damp dish towel and let rise in a warm place for 30 minutes, until the dough has reached the top of the pan.

4 Preheat the oven to 425°F/220°C. For the topping, lightly beat the egg white with the water in a bowl. Brush the top of the loaf with egg white glaze and sprinkle with the seeds. Bake for 30 minutes, until golden brown and the loaf sounds hollow when tapped on the bottom with your knuckles. Turn out onto a wire rack to cool.

crusty white bread

Ingredients

1 egg

1 egg yolk

³⁄₄–1 cup lukewarm water

*4½ cups white bread flour,
plus extra for dusting*

1½ tsp salt

2 tsp superfine sugar

1 tsp active dry yeast

2 tbsp butter, diced

vegetable oil, for brushing

MAKES 1 MEDIUM LOAF

1 Lightly beat together the egg and egg yolk in a measuring cup. Stir in enough lukewarm water to make up to 1¼ cups.

2 Sift the flour and salt together into a bowl and stir in the sugar and yeast. Add the butter and rub it in with your fingertips until the mixture resembles breadcrumbs. Make a well in the center, pour in the egg mixture, and stir well with a wooden spoon until the dough begins to come together, then knead with your hands until it leaves the side of the bowl. Turn out onto a lightly floured counter and knead well for about 10 minutes, until smooth and elastic.

3 Brush a bowl with oil. Shape the dough into a ball, put it into the bowl, and put the bowl into a plastic bag or cover with a damp dish towel. Let rise in a warm place for 1–2 hours, until the dough has doubled in volume.

4 Brush a 7½ x 4½ x 3½-inch/19 x 12 x 9-cm loaf pan with oil. Turn out the dough onto a lightly floured counter, punch down with your fist, and knead for 1 minute. With lightly floured hands, shape the dough into a rectangle the same length as the pan and flatten slightly. Fold it lengthwise into 3 and place in the prepared pan, seam side down. Put the pan into a plastic bag or cover with a damp dish towel and let rise in a warm place for 30 minutes, until the dough has reached the top of the pan.

5 Preheat the oven to 425°F/220°C. Bake the loaf for 30 minutes, until it has shrunk from the sides of the pan, is golden brown, and sounds hollow when tapped on the bottom with your knuckles. Turn out onto a wire rack to cool.

whole wheat harvest bread

Ingredients

2 cups whole wheat bread flour, plus extra for dusting

1 tsp salt

1 tbsp nonfat dry milk

2 tbsp soft brown sugar

1 tsp active dry yeast

1½ tbsp vegetable oil, plus extra for brushing

¾ cup lukewarm water

MAKES 1 SMALL LOAF

1 Sift the flour and salt together into a bowl, tip in the bran from the sifter, and stir in the milk, sugar, and yeast. Make a well in the center and pour in the oil and lukewarm water. Stir well with a wooden spoon until the dough begins to come together, then knead with your hands until it leaves the side of the bowl. Turn out onto a lightly floured counter and knead well for about 10 minutes, until smooth and elastic.

2 Brush a bowl with oil. Shape the dough into a ball, put it into the bowl, and put the bowl into a plastic bag or cover with a damp dish towel. Let rise in a warm place for 1 hour, until the dough has doubled in volume.

3 Brush a 6½ x 4¼ x 3¼-inch/17 x 11 x 8-cm loaf pan with oil. Turn out the dough onto a lightly floured counter, punch down with your fist, and knead for 1 minute. With lightly floured hands, shape the dough into a rectangle the same length as the pan and flatten slightly. Fold it lengthwise into 3 and place in the prepared pan, seam side down. Put the pan into a plastic bag or cover with a damp dish towel and let rise in a warm place for 30 minutes, until the dough has reached the top of the pan.

4 Preheat the oven to 425°F/220°C. Bake the loaf for about 30 minutes, until it has shrunk from the sides of the pan, the crust is golden brown, and it sounds hollow when tapped on the bottom with your knuckles. Turn out onto a wire rack to cool.

irish soda bread

Ingredients

vegetable oil, for brushing

4 cups all-purpose flour, plus extra for dusting

1 tsp salt

1 tsp baking soda

1¾ cups buttermilk

MAKES 1 LOAF

1 Preheat the oven to 425°F/220°C. Brush a cookie sheet with oil.

2 Sift the flour, salt, and baking soda together into a bowl. Make a well in the center and pour in most of the buttermilk. Mix well, first with a wooden spoon and then with your hands. The dough should be very soft but not too wet. If necessary, add the remaining buttermilk.

3 Turn out the dough onto a lightly floured counter and knead lightly and briefly. Shape into an 8-inch/20-cm round. Put the loaf onto the prepared cookie sheet and cut a cross in the top with a sharp knife.

4 Bake for 25–30 minutes, until golden brown and the loaf sounds hollow when tapped on the bottom with your knuckles. Transfer to a wire rack to cool slightly and serve warm.

hamburger buns

Ingredients

4 cups white bread flour, plus extra for dusting

1½ tsp salt

2 tsp superfine sugar

1 tsp active dry yeast

⅔ cup lukewarm water

⅔ cup lukewarm milk, plus extra for brushing

vegetable oil, for brushing

2–3 tbsp sesame seeds

MAKES 8 BUNS

1 Sift the flour and salt together into a bowl and stir in the sugar and yeast. Make a well in the center and pour in the lukewarm water and milk. Stir well with a wooden spoon until the dough begins to come together, then knead with your hands until it leaves the side of the bowl. Turn out onto a lightly floured counter and knead well for about 10 minutes, until smooth and elastic.

2 Brush a bowl with oil. Shape the dough into a ball, put it into the bowl, and put the bowl into a plastic bag or cover with a damp dish towel. Let rise in a warm place for 1 hour, until the dough has doubled in volume.

3 Brush 2 cookie sheets with oil. Turn out the dough onto a lightly floured counter and punch down with your fist. Divide it into 8 equal pieces, shape each into a ball, and put them on the prepared cookie sheets. Flatten slightly with a lightly floured hand and put the cookie sheets into plastic bags or cover with damp dish towels. Let rise in a warm place for 30 minutes.

4 Preheat the oven to 400°F/200°C. Lightly press the center of each bun with your fingers to release any large air bubbles. Brush the tops with milk and sprinkle with sesame seeds. Bake for 15–20 minutes, until light golden brown. Transfer to wire racks to cool.

gourmet bread

banana & orange bread

Ingredients

4½ cups white bread flour,
plus extra for dusting

1 tsp salt

1 tsp superfine sugar

1 tsp active dry yeast

3 tbsp unsalted butter, diced

1 large or 2 medium ripe
bananas

3 tbsp honey

4 tbsp orange juice

scant 1 cup lukewarm
buttermilk

vegetable oil, for brushing

milk, for glazing (optional)

MAKES 1 MEDIUM LOAF

1 Sift the flour and salt together into a bowl and stir in the sugar and yeast. Add the butter and rub in with your fingertips. Mash the bananas in another bowl with a fork and add to the mixture with the honey. Mix well and make a well in the center. Pour in the orange juice and buttermilk and stir well with a wooden spoon until the dough begins to come together, then knead with your hands until it leaves the side of the bowl.

2 Turn out onto a lightly floured counter and knead for 5–7 minutes, until smooth and elastic. If necessary, knead in a little more flour if the ripe bananas have made the dough very sticky. Brush a bowl with oil. Shape the dough into a ball, put it into the bowl, and put the bowl into a plastic bag or cover with a damp dish towel. Let rise in a warm place for 1 hour, until the dough has doubled in volume.

3 Brush a 9 x 5 x 3-inch/23 x 13 x 8-cm loaf pan with oil. Turn out the dough onto a lightly floured counter, punch down with your fist, and knead for 1 minute. With lightly floured hands, shape the dough into a rectangle the same length as the pan. Flatten slightly, fold it lengthwise into 3, and place in the prepared pan, seam side down. Put the pan into a plastic bag or cover with a damp dish towel and let rise in a warm place for 30 minutes, until the dough has reached the top of the pan.

4 Preheat the oven to 425°F/220°C. Brush the top of the loaf with milk, if using, and bake for 30 minutes, until it has shrunk from the sides of the pan, the crust is golden brown, and it sounds hollow when tapped on the bottom with your knuckles. Turn out onto a wire rack to cool.

orange marmalade loaf

Ingredients

4 cups white bread flour,
plus extra for dusting

1½ tsp salt

1½ tsp superfine sugar

1½ tsp active dry yeast

⅔ cup lukewarm water

⅔ cup lukewarm milk

2 tbsp vegetable oil, plus extra
for brushing

7 tbsp orange marmalade

Topping

1 egg yolk

1 tbsp milk

1 tbsp superfine sugar

1–2 tbsp candied orange peel

MAKES 1 LOAF

1 Sift the flour and salt together into a bowl and stir in the sugar and yeast. Make a well in the center and pour in the lukewarm water and milk. Stir well with a wooden spoon until the dough begins to come together, then knead with your hands until it leaves the side of the bowl. Turn out onto a lightly floured counter and knead well for about 10 minutes, until smooth and elastic.

2 Brush a bowl with oil. Shape the dough into a ball, put it into the bowl, and put the bowl into a plastic bag or cover with a damp dish towel. Let rise in a warm place for 1–2 hours, until the dough has doubled in volume.

3 Brush a 7½ x 4½ x 3½-inch/19 x 12 x 9-cm loaf pan with oil. Turn out the dough onto a lightly floured counter and punch down with your fist. Roll out to a rectangle about ¾ inch/2 cm thick. Spread the marmalade evenly over the dough leaving a ½-inch/1-cm border along one long side. Roll up the dough like a jelly roll and put it into the prepared pan, seam side down. Put the pan into a plastic bag or cover with a damp dish towel and let rise in a warm place for 45 minutes.

4 Preheat the oven to 425°F/220°C. To make the topping, beat the egg yolk with the milk and sugar in a bowl and brush it over the top of the loaf. Score the top and sprinkle with the orange peel. Bake for 25–30 minutes, until golden brown. Turn out onto a wire rack to cool.

bran & yogurt bread

Ingredients

1¾ cups white bread flour, plus extra for dusting

generous 1¼ cups whole wheat bread flour

1 tsp salt

¾ tsp active dry yeast

2 tbsp wheat bran

⅔ cup lukewarm water

½ cup plain yogurt

1 tbsp vegetable oil, plus extra for brushing

1 tbsp molasses or light corn syrup

MAKES 1 SMALL LOAF

1 Sift both types of flour and the salt together into a bowl and tip in the bran from the sifter. Stir in the yeast and wheat bran. Make a well in the center and pour in the lukewarm water, yogurt, oil, and molasses. Stir well with a wooden spoon until the dough begins to come together, then knead with your hands until it leaves the side of the bowl. Turn out onto a lightly floured counter and knead well for about 10 minutes, until smooth and elastic.

2 Brush a bowl with oil. Shape the dough into a ball, put it into the bowl, and put the bowl into a plastic bag or cover with a damp dish towel. Let rise in a warm place for 1–2 hours, until the dough has doubled in volume.

3 Brush a cookie sheet with oil. Turn out the dough onto a lightly floured counter, punch down with your fist, and knead for 1 minute. With lightly floured hands, shape the dough into a ball, and flatten slightly. Put the loaf onto the prepared cookie sheet. Put the cookie sheet into a plastic bag or cover with a damp dish towel and let rise in a warm place for 30 minutes.

4 Preheat the oven to 425°F/220°C. Slash the top of the loaf and bake for 30 minutes, until golden brown and it sounds hollow when tapped on the bottom with your knuckles. Transfer to a wire rack to cool.

granola bread

Ingredients

generous 2½ cups white bread flour, plus extra for dusting

¾ cup whole wheat bread flour

1½ tsp salt

generous 1¼ cups unsweetened granola

3 tbsp nonfat dry milk

1½ tsp active dry yeast

1 cup lukewarm water

2 tbsp vegetable oil, plus extra for brushing

1 tbsp honey

⅓ cup chopped plumped dried apricots

MAKES 1 LOAF

1 Sift both types of flour and the salt together into a bowl and tip in the bran from the sifter. Stir in the granola, milk, and yeast. Make a well in the center and pour in the lukewarm water, oil, and honey. Stir well with a wooden spoon until the dough begins to come together, then knead with your hands until it leaves the side of the bowl. Turn out onto a lightly floured counter and knead well for 5 minutes. Knead in the apricots and continue to knead for 5 minutes more, until the dough is smooth and elastic.

2 Brush a bowl with oil. Shape the dough into a ball, put it into the bowl, and put the bowl into a plastic bag or cover with a damp dish towel. Let rise in a warm place for 1 hour, until the dough has doubled in volume.

3 Brush a cookie sheet with oil. Turn out the dough onto a lightly floured surface and punch down with your fist. With lightly floured hands, shape the dough into a round and place on the prepared cookie sheet. Cut a cross in the top of the loaf. Put the cookie sheet into a plastic bag or cover with a damp dish towel and let rise in a warm place for 30–40 minutes.

4 Preheat the oven to 400°F/200°C. Bake the loaf for 30–35 minutes, until golden brown and it sounds hollow when tapped on the bottom with your knuckles. Transfer to a wire rack to cool.

rye bread

Ingredients

4 cups rye flour

2 cups white bread flour,
plus extra for dusting

2 tsp salt

2 tsp brown sugar

1½ tsp active dry yeast

scant 2 cups lukewarm water

2 tsp vegetable oil, plus extra
for brushing

Glaze

1 egg white

1 tbsp water

MAKES 1 LARGE LOAF

1 Sift the flours and salt together into a bowl. Add the sugar and yeast and stir to mix. Make a well in the center and pour in the lukewarm water and oil. Stir with a wooden spoon until the dough begins to come together, then knead with your hands until it leaves the side of the bowl. Turn out onto a lightly floured counter and knead for 10 minutes, until elastic and smooth.

2 Brush a bowl with oil. Shape the dough into a ball, put it into the bowl, and put the bowl into a plastic bag or cover with a damp dish towel. Let rise in a warm place for 2 hours, until the dough has doubled in volume.

3 Brush a cookie sheet with oil. Turn out the dough onto a lightly floured counter and punch down with your fist, then knead for 10 minutes more. Shape the dough into a ball, put it on the prepared cookie sheet, and put the cookie sheet in a plastic bag or cover with a damp dish towel. Let rise in a warm place for 40 minutes more, until the dough has doubled in volume.

4 Meanwhile, preheat the oven to 375°F/190°C. Beat the egg white with the water in a bowl. Bake the loaf for 20 minutes, then remove from the oven, and brush the top with the egg white glaze. Return to the oven and bake for 20 minutes more. Brush the top of the loaf with the glaze again and return to the oven for 20–30 minutes, until the crust is a rich brown color and the loaf sounds hollow when tapped on the bottom with your knuckles. Transfer to a wire rack to cool.

multigrain cheese bread

Ingredients

3½ cups white bread flour, plus extra for dusting

½ cup multigrain flour

1 tsp salt

2 tsp sugar

1½ tsp active dry yeast

5 tbsp ricotta cheese, beaten

1 egg, lightly beaten

generous ¾ cup lukewarm water

¾ cup grated Emmental cheese

3 oz/85 g Gorgonzola cheese, finely diced

3 tbsp finely chopped fresh chives

vegetable oil, for brushing

2 tbsp freshly grated Parmesan cheese

MAKES 1 LOAF

1 Sift both types of flour and the salt together into a bowl and stir in the sugar and yeast. Make a well in the center and add the ricotta, egg, and lukewarm water. Stir well with a wooden spoon until the dough begins to come together. Add the Emmental cheese, Gorgonzola cheese, and chives and knead with your hands until fully incorporated and the dough comes away from the side of the bowl. Turn out onto a lightly floured counter and knead well for about 10 minutes, until smooth and elastic.

2 Brush a bowl with oil. Shape the dough into a ball, put it into the bowl, and put the bowl into a plastic bag or cover with a damp dish towel. Let rise in a warm place for 1 hour, until the dough has doubled in volume.

3 Brush a cookie sheet with oil. Turn out the dough onto a lightly floured counter and punch down with your fist. With lightly floured hands, shape into an 8-inch/20-cm round and place on the prepared cookie sheet. Put the cookie sheet into a plastic bag or cover with a damp dish towel and let rise in a warm place for 40–45 minutes.

4 Preheat the oven to 400°F/200°C. Sprinkle the Parmesan cheese over the loaf and bake for 40–45 minutes, until golden brown and it sounds hollow when tapped on the bottom with your knuckles. Transfer to a wire rack to cool.

sourdough bread

Ingredients

4 cups rye flour

4 cups whole wheat flour

4 tsp salt

1½ cups lukewarm water

2 tbsp molasses

1 tbsp vegetable oil, plus extra
for brushing

all-purpose flour, for dusting

Starter

¾ cup whole wheat flour

¾ cup white bread flour

generous ¼ cup superfine
sugar

1 cup milk

MAKES 2 LOAVES

1 First, make the starter. Put the flours, sugar, and milk into a
nonmetallic bowl and beat well with a fork. Cover with a damp dish
towel and let stand at room temperature for 4–5 days, until the mixture
is frothy and smells sour.

2 Sift both types of flour and half the salt together into a bowl and add
the lukewarm water, molasses, oil, and starter. Mix well with a wooden
spoon until a dough begins to form, then knead with your hands until it
leaves the side of the bowl. Turn out onto a lightly floured counter and
knead for 10 minutes, until smooth and elastic.

3 Brush a bowl with oil. Form the dough into a ball, put it into the bowl,
and put the bowl into a plastic bag or cover with a damp dish towel. Let
rise in a warm place for 2 hours, until doubled in volume.

4 Dust 2 cookie sheets with flour. Mix the remaining salt with
4 tablespoons of water in a bowl. Turn out the dough onto a lightly floured
counter and punch down with your fist, then knead for 10 minutes more.
Halve the dough, shape each piece into an oval, and place the loaves on
the prepared cookie sheets. Brush with the salt-water glaze and let stand
in a warm place, brushing frequently with the glaze, for 30 minutes.

5 Preheat the oven to 425°F/220°C. Brush the loaves with the remaining
glaze and bake for 30 minutes, until the crust is golden brown and they
sound hollow when tapped on the bottom with your knuckles. If it is
necessary to cook them for longer, reduce the oven temperature to
375°F/190°C. Transfer to wire racks to cool.

braided poppy seed bread

Ingredients

2 cups white bread flour, plus extra for dusting

1 tsp salt

2 tbsp nonfat dry milk

1½ tbsp superfine sugar

1 tsp active dry yeast

¾ cup lukewarm water

2 tbsp vegetable oil, plus extra for brushing

5 tbsp poppy seeds

Topping

1 egg yolk

1 tbsp milk

1 tbsp superfine sugar

2 tbsp poppy seeds

MAKES 1 LOAF

1 Sift the flour and salt together into a bowl and stir in the milk, sugar, and yeast. Make a well in the center and pour in the lukewarm water and oil. Stir well with a wooden spoon until the dough begins to come together. Add the poppy seeds and knead with your hands until they are fully incorporated and the dough leaves the side of the bowl. Turn out onto a lightly floured counter and knead well for about 10 minutes, until smooth and elastic.

2 Brush a bowl with oil. Shape the dough into a ball, put it into the bowl, and put the bowl into a plastic bag or cover with a damp dish towel. Let rise in a warm place for 1 hour, until the dough has doubled in volume.

3 Brush a cookie sheet with oil. Turn out the dough onto a lightly floured surface, punch down with your fist, and knead for 1–2 minutes. Divide the dough into 3 equal pieces and shape each into a rope 10–12 inches/25–30 cm long. Place the ropes side by side and press them together at one end. Braid the dough, pinch the other end together, and tuck it underneath. Put the loaf on the prepared cookie sheet. Put the cookie sheet in a plastic bag or cover with a damp dish towel and let rise in a warm place for 30 minutes.

4 Preheat the oven to 400°F/200°C. To make the topping, beat the egg yolk with the milk and sugar. Brush the egg glaze over the top of the loaf and sprinkle with the poppy seeds. Bake for 30–35 minutes, until golden brown and the loaf sounds hollow when tapped on the bottom with your knuckles. Transfer to a wire rack to cool.

pita breads

Ingredients

3 cups white bread flour, plus extra for dusting

1½ tsp salt

1 tsp superfine sugar

1 tsp active dry yeast

1 tbsp olive oil, plus extra for brushing

scant 1 cup lukewarm water

MAKES 6–8 PITA BREADS

1 Sift the flour and salt together into a bowl and stir in the sugar and yeast. Make a well in the center and pour in the oil and lukewarm water. Stir well with a wooden spoon until the dough begins to come together, then knead with your hands until it leaves the side of the bowl. Turn out onto a lightly floured counter and knead well for about 10 minutes, until smooth and elastic.

2 Brush a bowl with oil. Shape the dough into a ball, put it into the bowl, and put the bowl into a plastic bag or cover with a damp dish towel. Let rise in a warm place for 1 hour, until the dough has doubled in volume.

3 Turn out onto a lightly floured counter and punch down with your fist. Divide the dough into 6 or 8 equal pieces, shape each piece into a ball, and place on a cookie sheet. Put the sheet into a plastic bag or cover with a damp dish towel and let rest for 10 minutes.

4 With floured hands, slightly flatten a dough ball and roll out on a lightly floured surface to an oval about 6 inches/15 cm long and 1/4 inches/5 mm thick. Place on a lightly floured dish towel, sprinkle lightly with flour, and cover with another dish towel. Repeat with the remaining dough balls and let rise for 30 minutes.

5 Meanwhile, put 2 or 3 cookie sheets in the oven and preheat to 450°F/230°C. Transfer the pita breads to the heated cookie sheets, spacing them well apart, and bake for 5 minutes, until puffed up and golden brown. Transfer to wire racks to cool slightly, then cover with a dish towel to keep them soft.

regional bread

tomato & rosemary focaccia

Ingredients

4½ cups white bread flour, plus extra for dusting

1½ tsp salt

1½ tsp active dry yeast

2 tbsp chopped fresh rosemary, plus extra sprigs to garnish

6 tbsp extra virgin olive oil, plus extra for brushing

1¼ cups lukewarm water

6 oven-dried or sun-blush tomato halves

1 tsp coarse sea salt

MAKES 1 LOAF

1 Sift the flour and salt together into a bowl and stir in the yeast and rosemary. Make a well in the center, pour in 4 tablespoons of the oil, and mix quickly with a wooden spoon. Gradually stir in the lukewarm water but do not overmix. Turn out onto a lightly floured counter and knead for 2 minutes. The dough will be quite wet; do not add more flour.

2 Brush a bowl with oil. Shape the dough into a ball, put it into the bowl, and put the bowl into a plastic bag or cover with a damp dish towel. Let rise in a warm place for 2 hours, until doubled in volume.

3 Brush a cookie sheet with oil. Turn out the dough onto a lightly floured counter and punch down with your fist, then knead for 1 minute. Put the dough onto the prepared cookie sheet and press out into an even layer. Put the cookie sheet into a plastic bag or cover with a damp dish towel. Let rise in a warm place for 1 hour.

4 Preheat the oven to 475°F/240°C. Cut the tomato halves in half. Whisk the remaining oil with a little water in a bowl. Dip your fingers into the oil mixture and press them into the dough to make dimples all over the loaf. Sprinkle with the sea salt. Press the tomato quarters into some of the dimples, drizzle with the remaining oil mixture, and sprinkle the loaf with the rosemary sprigs.

5 Reduce the oven temperature to 425°F/220°C and bake the focaccia for 20 minutes, until golden brown. Transfer to a wire rack to cool slightly, then serve while still warm. Alternatively, let the loaf cool completely and reheat in a low oven before serving.

ciabatta

Ingredients

1¾ cups lukewarm water

4 tbsp lukewarm lowfat milk

4½ cups white bread flour

1 envelope active dry yeast

2 tsp salt

3 tbsp olive oil

Biga

3 cups white bread flour, plus
extra for dusting

1¼ tsp active dry yeast

scant 1 cup lukewarm water

MAKES 3 LOAVES

1 First, make the biga. Sift the flour into a bowl, stir in the yeast, and make a well in the center. Pour in the lukewarm water and stir until the dough comes together. Turn out onto a lightly floured counter and knead for 5 minutes, until smooth and elastic. Shape the dough into a ball, put it into a bowl, and put the bowl into a plastic bag or cover with a damp dish towel. Let rise in a warm place for 12 hours, until just beginning to collapse.

2 Gradually mix the water and milk into the biga, beating with a wooden spoon. Gradually mix in the flour and yeast with your hand, adding them a little at a time. Finally, mix in the salt and oil with your hand. The dough will be very wet; do not add extra flour. Put the bowl into a plastic bag or cover with a damp dish towel and let the dough rise in a warm place for 2 hours, until doubled in volume.

3 Dust 3 cookie sheets with flour. Using a spatula, divide the dough among the prepared cookie sheets without knocking out the air. With lightly floured hands, gently pull and shape each piece of dough into a rectangular loaf, then flatten slightly. Dust the tops of the loaves with flour and let rise in a warm place for 30 minutes.

4 Meanwhile, preheat the oven to 425°F/220°C. Bake the loaves for 25–30 minutes, until the crust is lightly golden and the loaves sound hollow when tapped on the bottom with your knuckles. Transfer to wire racks to cool.

baguettes

Ingredients

4 cups white bread flour, plus extra for dusting

1½ tsp salt

1½ tsp active dry yeast

1⅓ cups lukewarm water

vegetable oil, for brushing

MAKES 2 BAGUETTES

1 Sift the flour and salt together into a bowl and stir in the yeast. Make a well in the center and pour in the lukewarm water. Stir well with a wooden spoon until the dough begins to come together, then knead with your hands until it leaves the side of the bowl. Turn out onto a lightly floured counter and knead well for about 10 minutes, until smooth and elastic.

2 Brush a bowl with oil. Shape the dough into a ball, put it into the bowl, and put the bowl into a plastic bag or cover with a damp dish towel. Let rise in a warm place for 1 hour, until the dough has doubled in volume.

3 Turn out the dough onto a lightly floured counter, punch down with your fist, and knead for 1–2 minutes. Cut the dough in half and shape each piece into a ball. Roll out each ball to a rectangle measuring 3 x 8 inches/7.5 x 20 cm. From one long side of a dough rectangle, fold one third of the dough down, then fold over the remaining third of the dough. Press gently. Fold the second dough rectangle in the same way. Put both loaves in plastic bags or cover with damp dish towels and let rest for 10 minutes. Repeat the rolling and folding twice more, letting the dough rest for 10 minutes each time.

4 Lightly flour and pleat 2 dish towels or flour 2 bannetons (lined French bread baskets). Gently roll and stretch each piece of dough until it is 12 inches/30 cm long and an even thickness. Support each loaf on the pleated dish towels or in the bannetons, cover with damp dish towels, and let rise for 30–40 minutes.

5 Preheat the oven to 450°F/230°C. Brush 1 or 2 cookie sheets with oil. Carefully roll the loaves onto the cookie sheets and slash the tops several times with a sharp knife. Spray the oven with water (see page 10) and bake the loaves for 15–20 minutes, until golden brown. Transfer to a wire rack to cool.

olive & sun-dried tomato bread

Ingredients

3½ cups all-purpose flour, plus extra for dusting

1 tsp salt

1 envelope active dry yeast

1 tsp brown sugar

1 tbsp chopped fresh thyme

scant 1 cup lukewarm water

4 tbsp olive oil, plus extra for brushing

½ cup black olives, pitted and sliced

½ cup green olives, pitted and sliced

1¾ cups drained sun-dried tomatoes in oil, sliced

1 egg yolk, beaten

MAKES 2 LOAVES

1 Sift the flour and salt together into a bowl and stir in the yeast, sugar, and thyme. Make a well in the center and pour in the lukewarm water and oil. Stir well with a wooden spoon until the dough begins to come together, then knead with your hands until it leaves the side of the bowl. Turn out onto a lightly floured counter and knead in the olives and sun-dried tomatoes, then knead for 5 minutes more, until the dough is smooth and elastic.

2 Brush a bowl with oil. Shape the dough into a ball, put it into the bowl, and put the bowl into a plastic bag or cover with a damp dish towel. Let rise in a warm place for 1–1½ hours, until the dough has doubled in volume.

3 Dust a cookie sheet with flour. Turn out the dough onto a lightly floured counter and punch down with your fist. Cut it in half and with lightly floured hands, shape each half into a round or oval. Put them on the prepared cookie sheet and put the cookie sheet into a plastic bag or cover with a damp dish towel. Let rise in a warm place for 45 minutes.

4 Preheat the oven to 400°F/200°C. Make 3 shallow diagonal slashes on the top of each loaf and brush with the beaten egg yolk. Bake for 40 minutes, until golden brown and the loaves sound hollow when tapped on the bottom with your knuckles. Transfer to a wire rack to cool.

flatbread with onion & rosemary

Ingredients

4 cups white bread flour, plus extra for dusting

½ tsp salt

1½ tsp active dry yeast

2 tbsp chopped fresh rosemary, plus small sprigs to garnish

5 tbsp extra virgin olive oil, plus extra for brushing

1¼ cups lukewarm water

1 red onion, thinly sliced and pushed out into rings

1 tbsp coarse sea salt

MAKES 1 LOAF

1 Sift the flour and salt together into a bowl and stir in the yeast and rosemary. Make a well in the center and pour in 3 tablespoons of the oil and all of the lukewarm water. Stir well with a wooden spoon until the dough begins to come together, then knead with your hands until it leaves the side of the bowl. Turn out onto a lightly floured counter and knead well for about 10 minutes, until smooth and elastic.

2 Brush a bowl with oil. Shape the dough into a ball, put it into the bowl, and put the bowl into a plastic bag or cover with a damp dish towel. Let rise in a warm place for 1 hour, until the dough has doubled in volume.

3 Brush a cookie sheet with oil. Turn out the dough onto a lightly floured counter, punch down with your fist, and knead for 1 minute. Roll out the dough to a round about 12 inches/30 cm in diameter and put it on the prepared cookie sheet. Put the cookie sheet into a plastic bag or cover with a damp dish towel and let rise in a warm place for 20–30 minutes.

4 Preheat the oven to 400°F/200°C. Using the handle of a wooden spoon, make indentations all over the surface of the loaf. Spread the onion rings over the top, drizzle with the remaining oil, and sprinkle with the sea salt. Bake for 20 minutes. Sprinkle with the rosemary sprigs, return to the oven, and bake for 5 minutes more, until golden brown. Transfer to a wire rack to cool slightly and serve warm.

cilantro & garlic naan

Ingredients

2½ cups white bread flour, plus extra for dusting

1 tsp salt

1 tbsp ground cilantro

1 garlic clove, very finely chopped

1 tsp active dry yeast

2 tsp honey

scant ½ cup lukewarm water

4 tbsp plain yogurt

1 tbsp vegetable oil, plus extra for brushing

1 tsp black onion seeds

1 tbsp chopped fresh cilantro

MAKES 3 NAAN

1 Sift the flour, salt, and coriander together into a bowl and stir in the garlic and yeast. Make a well in the center and pour in the honey, lukewarm water, yogurt, and oil. Stir well with a wooden spoon until the dough begins to come together, then knead with your hands until it leaves the side of the bowl. Turn out onto a lightly floured counter and knead well for about 10 minutes, until smooth and elastic.

2 Brush a bowl with oil. Shape the dough into a ball, put it into the bowl, and put the bowl into a plastic bag or cover with a damp dish towel. Let rise in a warm place for 1–2 hours, until the dough has doubled in volume.

3 Put 3 cookie sheets into the oven and preheat to 475°F/240°C. Preheat the broiler. Turn out the dough onto a lightly floured counter and punch down with your fist. Divide the dough into 3 pieces, shape each piece into a ball, and cover 2 of them with oiled plastic wrap. Roll out the uncovered piece of dough into a teardrop shape about 3/8 inch/8 mm thick and cover with oiled plastic wrap. Roll out the other pieces of dough in the same way. Place the flatbreads on the hot cookie sheets and sprinkle with the onion seeds and chopped cilantro. Bake for 5 minutes, until puffed up. Transfer the naan to the broiler pan, brush with oil, and broil for 2–3 minutes. Serve warm.

greek olive & feta bread

Ingredients

3¼ cups white bread flour, plus extra for dusting

1 tsp salt

1½ tsp superfine sugar

1 tbsp nonfat dry milk

1 tsp active dry yeast

scant 1 cup lukewarm water

½ cup pitted black olives, chopped

2 oz/55 g feta cheese, crumbled

2 tbsp olive oil, plus extra for brushing

1 tsp chopped fresh thyme

½ tsp dried oregano

MAKES 1 LOAF

1 Sift the flour and salt together into a bowl and stir in the sugar, milk, and yeast. Make a well in the center and pour in the lukewarm water. Stir well with a wooden spoon until the dough begins to come together, then knead with your hands until it leaves the side of the bowl. Turn out onto a lightly floured counter and knead in the olives and feta, then knead for 5 minutes more, until the dough is smooth and elastic.

2 Brush a bowl with oil. Shape the dough into a ball, put it into the bowl, and put the bowl into a plastic bag or cover with a damp dish towel. Let rise in a warm place for 1 hour, until the dough has doubled in volume.

3 Brush an 8-inch/20-cm round cake pan with oil. Turn out the dough onto a lightly floured counter and punch down with your fist. With lightly floured hands, shape it into an 8-inch/20-cm round loaf and put it into the prepared pan. Put the pan into a plastic bag or cover with a damp dish towel and let rise in a warm place for 40–45 minutes.

4 Preheat the oven to 400°F/200°C. Brush the top of the loaf with the olive oil and sprinkle with the herbs. Bake for 35–40 minutes, until golden brown. Turn out onto a wire rack to cool.

garlic & sage bread

Ingredients

2 ¼ cups whole wheat bread flour, plus extra for dusting

1 envelope active dry yeast

3 tbsp chopped fresh sage

2 tsp sea salt

3 garlic cloves, finely chopped

1 tsp honey

⅔ cup lukewarm water

vegetable oil, for brushing

MAKES 1 LOAF

1 Sift the flour into a bowl and tip in the bran from the sifter. Stir in the yeast, sage, and half the salt. Reserve 1 teaspoon of the garlic and stir the remainder into the bowl. Make a well in the center and pour in the honey and lukewarm water. Stir well with a wooden spoon until the dough begins to come together, then knead with your hands until it leaves the side of the bowl. Turn out onto a lightly floured counter and knead well for about 10 minutes, until smooth and elastic.

2 Brush a bowl with oil. Shape the dough into a ball, put it into the bowl, and put the bowl into a plastic bag or cover with a damp dish towel. Let rise in a warm place for 1 hour, until the dough has doubled in volume.

3 Brush a cookie sheet with oil. Turn out the dough onto a lightly floured counter, punch down with your fist, and knead for 2 minutes. Roll the dough into a long sausage, shape into a ring, and put it onto the prepared cookie sheet. Brush the outside of a bowl with oil and put it into the center of the ring to prevent it from closing up while the dough is rising. Put the cookie sheet into a plastic bag or cover with a damp dish towel and let rise in a warm place for 30 minutes.

4 Preheat the oven to 400°F/200°C. Remove the bowl from the center of the loaf. Sprinkle the loaf with the remaining salt and the reserved garlic and bake for 25–30 minutes, until golden brown and the loaf sounds hollow when tapped on the bottom with your knuckles. Transfer to a wire rack to cool.

cornbread

Ingredients

vegetable oil, for brushing

1½ cups all-purpose flour

1 tsp salt

4 tsp baking powder

1 tsp superfine sugar

2½ cups yellow cornmeal

½ cup butter, softened

4 eggs

1 cup milk

3 tbsp heavy cream

MAKES 1 SMALL LOAF

1 Preheat the oven to 400°F/200°C. Brush an 8-inch/20-cm square cake pan with oil.

2 Sift the flour, salt, and baking powder together into a bowl. Add the sugar and cornmeal and stir to mix. Add the butter and cut it into the dry ingredients with a knife, then rub in with your fingertips until the mixture resembles breadcrumbs.

3 Lightly beat the eggs with the milk and cream in a bowl, then stir into the cornmeal mixture until thoroughly combined.

4 Spoon the mixture into the prepared pan and smooth the surface. Bake for 30–35 minutes, until a toothpick inserted into the center of the loaf comes out clean. Remove the pan from the oven and let the bread cool for 5–10 minutes, then cut into squares and serve warm.

basic pizza dough

Ingredients

1½ cups all-purpose flour, plus extra for dusting

1 tsp salt

1 tsp active dry yeast

1 tbsp olive oil, plus extra for brushing and drizzling

6 tbsp lukewarm water

Topping

¾ cup prepared pizza tomato sauce or 12 oz/350 g tomatoes, peeled and halved

1 garlic clove, thinly sliced

2 oz/55 g mozzarella cheese, thinly sliced

1 tsp dried oregano

sprigs of fresh basil, to garnish

salt and pepper

MAKES 1 PIZZA

1 Sift the flour and salt together into a bowl and stir in the yeast. Make a well in the center and pour in the oil and lukewarm water. Stir well with a wooden spoon until the dough begins to come together, then knead with your hands until it leaves the side of the bowl. Turn out onto a lightly floured counter and knead well for 5–10 minutes, until smooth and elastic.

2 Brush a bowl with oil. Shape the dough into a ball, put it into the bowl, and put the bowl into a plastic bag or cover with a damp dish towel. Let rise in a warm place for 1 hour, until the dough has doubled in volume.

3 Brush a cookie sheet with oil. Turn out the dough onto a lightly floured counter, punch down with your fist, and knead for 1 minute. Roll or press out the dough to a 10-inch/25-cm round. Place on the prepared cookie sheet and push up the edge slightly all around. Put the cookie sheet in a plastic bag or cover with a damp dish towel and let rise in a warm place for 10 minutes.

4 Preheat the oven to 400°F/200°C. Spread the tomato sauce, if using, over the pizza bottom almost to the edge. If using fresh tomatoes, squeeze out some of the juice and coarsely chop the flesh. Spread them evenly over the pizza base and drizzle with oil. Sprinkle the garlic over the tomato, add the mozzarella cheese, sprinkle with the oregano, and season with salt and pepper. Bake for 15–20 minutes, until the crust is golden brown and crisp. Brush the crust with olive oil, garnish with fresh basil, and serve immediately.

turkish flatbreads

Ingredients

6½ cups all-purpose flour,
plus extra for dusting

1½ tsp salt

1 tsp ground cumin

½ tsp ground coriander

1 tsp superfine sugar

1 envelope active dry yeast

2 tbsp olive oil, plus extra
for brushing

1¾ cups lukewarm water

MAKES 8 FLATBREADS

1 Sift together the flour, salt, cumin, and coriander into a bowl and stir in the sugar and yeast. Make a well in the center and pour in the oil and lukewarm water. Stir well with a wooden spoon until the dough begins to come together, then knead with your hands until it leaves the side of the bowl. Turn out onto a lightly floured counter and knead well for about 10 minutes, until smooth and elastic.

2 Brush a bowl with oil. Shape the dough into a ball, put it into the bowl, and put the bowl into a plastic bag or cover with a damp dish towel. Let rise in a warm place for 1 hour, until the dough has doubled in volume.

3 Lightly brush a cookie sheet with oil. Turn out the dough onto a lightly floured counter, punch down with your fist, and knead for 1–2 minutes. Divide the dough into 8 equal pieces, shape each piece into a ball, then roll out to an 8-inch/20-cm round. Cover the rounds with a damp dish towel and let rest for 20 minutes.

4 Heat a heavy skillet and brush the bottom with oil. Add 1 dough round, cover, and cook for 2–3 minutes, until lightly browned on the underside. Turn over with a metal spatula, re-cover the skillet, and cook for 2 minutes more, until lightly browned on the second side. Remove from the skillet and cook the remaining dough rounds in the same way.

sweet bread

spicy cinnamon bread

Ingredients

¼ cup unsalted butter, plus extra for greasing

3 cups all-purpose flour

1½ tsp baking powder

¼ tsp salt

1 tsp ground cinnamon

½ tsp apple pie spice

½ tsp grated nutmeg

½ tsp ground ginger

4 tbsp molasses

3 eggs, lightly beaten

¼ cup milk

scant ¼ cup raisins

¼ cup chopped plumped dried apple

MAKES 1 SMALL LOAF

1 Preheat the oven to 350°F/180°C. Grease a 9 x 5 x 3-inch/23 x 13 x 8-cm loaf pan with butter. Sift the flour, baking powder, salt, cinnamon, apple pie spice, nutmeg, and ginger together into a bowl and set aside.

2 Put the butter and molasses into a small saucepan and heat gently, stirring continuously, until melted and smooth. Remove the pan from the heat and let cool slightly. Stir in the eggs, milk, raisins, and dried apple. Add the molasses mixture to the dry ingredients and stir gently with a wooden spoon until thoroughly combined.

3 Turn the mixture into the prepared pan and smooth the top. Bake for about 1 hour, until golden and firm and a toothpick inserted into the center of the loaf comes out clean. Let stand in the pan for 10 minutes, then turn out onto a wire rack to cool.

banana & cranberry loaf

Ingredients

butter, for greasing
scant 2 cups self-rising flour
$\frac{1}{2}$ tsp baking powder
generous $\frac{1}{2}$ cup brown sugar
2 bananas, mashed
$\frac{1}{3}$ cup chopped candied peel
$\frac{3}{4}$ cup chopped mixed nuts
$\frac{1}{3}$ cup dried cranberries
5–6 tbsp orange juice
2 eggs, lightly beaten
$\frac{2}{3}$ cup vegetable oil
$\frac{3}{4}$ cup confectioners' sugar
grated rind of 1 orange

MAKES 1 LOAF

1 Preheat the oven to 350°F/180°C. Grease a 9 x 5 x 3-inch/23 x 13 x 8-cm loaf pan with butter and line the bottom with parchment paper.

2 Sift the flour and baking powder together into a bowl and stir in the sugar, bananas, candied peel, nuts, and cranberries. Combine the orange juice, eggs, and oil in another bowl, then add to the dry ingredients. Stir well with a wooden spoon until thoroughly combined.

3 Spoon the mixture into the prepared loaf pan and smooth the top. Bake for 1 hour, until golden and firm and a toothpick inserted into the center of the loaf comes out clean. Turn out onto a wire rack to cool.

4 Mix the confectioners' sugar with a little water in a bowl and drizzle it over the cooled loaf. Sprinkle the orange rind on top and let set.

pecan honey bread

Ingredients

4½ cups white bread flour, plus extra for dusting

¾ tsp salt

1½ tbsp active dry yeast

3 tbsp unsalted butter

⅓ cup chopped pecans

1 tbsp grated orange rind

½ cup lukewarm milk

¾ cup mandarin or orange yogurt

3 tbsp honey

vegetable oil, for brushing

MAKES 1 LOAF

1 Sift the flour and salt together into a bowl and stir in the yeast. Add the butter and rub in with your fingertips, then stir in the nuts and orange rind. Make a well in the center and pour in the lukewarm milk, yogurt, and honey. Stir well with a wooden spoon until the dough begins to come together, then knead with your hands until it leaves the side of the bowl. Turn out onto a lightly floured counter and knead well for about 10 minutes, until smooth and elastic.

2 Brush a bowl with oil. Shape the dough into a ball, put it into the bowl, and put the bowl into a plastic bag or cover with a damp dish towel. Let rise in a warm place for 1 hour, until the dough has doubled in volume.

3 Brush a 9 x 5 x 3-inch/23 x 13 x 8-cm loaf pan with oil. Turn out the dough onto a lightly floured counter, knock back with your fist, and knead for 1 minute. With lightly floured hands, flatten the dough into a rectangle the same width as the pan. Fold it into 3 and place in the prepared pan, seam side down. Put the pan into a plastic bag or cover with a damp dish towel and let rise in a warm place for 30–40 minutes, until the dough has reached the top of the pan.

4 Meanwhile, preheat the oven to 450°F/230°C. Bake the loaf for 30–40 minutes, until it has shrunk from the sides of the pan, the crust is golden brown, and the loaf sounds hollow when tapped on the bottom with your knuckles. Turn out onto a wire rack to cool.

malted fruit loaf

Ingredients

3 cups all-purpose flour, plus extra for dusting

1 tsp salt

1 tsp active dry yeast

1 cup golden raisins

scant 1 cup lukewarm water

2 tsp vegetable oil, plus extra for brushing

2 tbsp malt extract

1½ tbsp molasses

MAKES 1 LOAF

1 Sift the flour and salt together into a bowl and stir in the yeast and golden raisins. Make a well in the center and pour in the lukewarm water, oil, malt extract, and molasses. Stir well with a wooden spoon until the dough begins to come together, then knead with your hands until it leaves the side of the bowl. Turn out onto a lightly floured counter and knead well for about 10 minutes, until smooth and elastic.

2 Brush a bowl with oil. Shape the dough into a ball, put it into the bowl, and put the bowl into a plastic bag or cover with a damp dish towel. Let rise in a warm place for 1–2 hours, until the dough has doubled in volume.

3 Brush a 9 x 5 x 3-inch/23 x 13 x 8-cm loaf pan with oil. Turn out the dough onto a lightly floured counter, knock back with your fist, and knead for 1 minute. With lightly floured hands, flatten the dough into a rectangle the same width as the pan. Fold it into 3 and place in the prepared pan, seam side down. Put the pan into a plastic bag or cover with a damp dish towel and let rise in a warm place for 30–40 minutes, until the dough has reached the top of the pan.

4 Meanwhile, preheat the oven to 450°F/230°C. Bake the loaf for 30–40 minutes, until it has shrunk from the sides of the pan, the crust is golden brown, and the loaf sounds hollow when tapped on the bottom with your knuckles. Turn out onto a wire rack to cool.

apple & apricot loaf

Ingredients

½ cup unsalted butter, softened, plus extra for greasing

generous ⅔ cup brown sugar

2 eggs, lightly beaten

⅓ cup plumped dried apricots, chopped

2 apples, peeled, cored, and coarsely grated

2 tbsp milk

1½ cups self-rising flour

1 tsp ground allspice

½ tsp ground cinnamon

MAKES 1 LOAF

1 Preheat the oven to 350°F/180°C. Grease a 9 x 5 x 3-inch/23 x 13 x 8-cm loaf pan with butter and line with parchment paper.

2 Cream the butter and sugar together in a bowl until light and fluffy. Gradually beat in the eggs. Reserve 1 tablespoon of the apricots and fold in the remainder with the apples and milk. Sift the flour, allspice, and cinnamon together into the bowl and fold into the mixture.

3 Spoon the mixture into the prepared pan and sprinkle the reserved apricots on top. Bake for 55–60 minutes, until risen and golden and a toothpick inserted into the center comes out clean. Let cool in the pan for 10 minutes, then turn out onto a wire rack, peel off the lining paper, and let cool completely.

strawberry jelly splits

Ingredients

2 cups white bread flour, plus extra for dusting

½ tsp salt

2 tbsp superfine sugar

1 tsp active dry yeast

⅔ cup lukewarm water

1 tbsp melted butter

vegetable oil, for brushing

confectioners' sugar, for dusting

Filling
strawberry jelly

stiffly whipped heavy cream

MAKES 8 SPLITS

1 Sift the flour and salt together into a bowl and stir in the superfine sugar and yeast. Make a well in the center and pour in the lukewarm water and melted butter. Stir well with a wooden spoon until the dough begins to come together, then knead with your hands until it leaves the side of the bowl. Turn out onto a lightly floured counter and knead well for about 10 minutes, until smooth and elastic.

2 Brush a bowl with oil. Shape the dough into a ball, put it into the bowl, and put the bowl into a plastic bag or cover with a damp dish towel. Let rise in a warm place for 1–1½ hours, until the dough has doubled in volume.

3 Brush 2 cookie sheets with oil. Turn out the dough onto a lightly floured counter and punch down with your fist. Divide the dough into 8 equal pieces, shape each piece into a ball, put them onto the prepared cookie sheets, and flatten slightly. Put the cookie sheets into plastic bags or cover with damp dish towels and let rise in a warm place for 45 minutes.

4 Preheat the oven to 425°F/220°C. Bake the buns for 15 minutes, until golden. Transfer to a wire rack to cool completely. To serve, split in half with a sharp knife, spread the bottom half with plenty of strawberry jelly, and top with a good spoonful of cream. Replace the tops, dust lightly with confectioners' sugar, and serve.

gingerbread

Ingredients

generous ⅔ cup butter, plus extra for greasing

¾ cup brown sugar

2 tbsp molasses

2 apples

1 tbsp lemon juice

2 cups all-purpose flour

1 tsp baking powder

2 tsp baking soda

2 tsp ground ginger

⅔ cup milk

1 egg, lightly beaten

MAKES 12 BARS

1 Preheat the oven to 325°F/160°C. Grease a 9-inch/23-cm square cake pan with butter and line with parchment paper.

2 Put the butter, sugar, and molasses into a saucepan and melt over low heat, stirring occasionally. Remove the pan from the heat and let cool.

3 Meanwhile, peel, core, and chop the apples, then toss with the lemon juice in a bowl and set aside. Sift the flour, baking powder, baking soda, and ground ginger into another bowl. Make a well in the center, add the milk, egg, and cooled butter mixture, and stir with a wooden spoon until thoroughly combined. Stir in the chopped apple.

4 Pour the mixture into the prepared pan and smooth the top. Bake for 30–35 minutes, until the gingerbread has risen and a toothpick inserted into the center comes out clean. Let cool in the pan before turning out and cutting into 12 bars.

italian chocolate chip bread

Ingredients

vegetable oil, for brushing

2 cups all-purpose flour, plus extra for dusting

1 tbsp unsweetened cocoa

pinch of salt

1 tbsp butter, plus ½ tsp melted butter for brushing

1 tbsp superfine sugar

1 envelope active dry yeast

⅔ cup lukewarm water

⅓ cup semisweet chocolate chips

MAKES 1 LOAF

1 Brush a cookie sheet with oil. Sift the flour, cocoa, and salt together into a bowl. Add the butter and cut it into the dry ingredients, then stir in the sugar and yeast.

2 Gradually add the lukewarm water, stirring well with a wooden spoon until the dough begins to come together, then knead with your hands until it leaves the side of the bowl. Turn out onto a lightly floured counter and knead for about 10 minutes, until smooth and elastic.

3 Knead the chocolate chips into the dough, then form into a round loaf. Put the loaf onto the prepared cookie sheet and put the cookie sheet into a plastic bag or cover with a damp dish towel. Let rise in a warm place for 1–1½ hours, until doubled in volume.

4 Preheat the oven to 425°F/220°C. Bake the loaf for 10 minutes, then reduce the oven temperature to 375°F/190°C, and bake for 15 minutes more.

5 Transfer the loaf to a wire rack and brush the top with the melted butter. Cover with a dish towel and let cool.